<u>Dedication</u>

I would like to thank my friends and my wife for their continued support. I hope this book truly makes your life better and easier.

This book was written by Daniel Melehi with the A.I assistance of Inventabot.com

Daniel Melehi

© May 2023

Contents

3

Introduction to Flutter

Flutter is an open-source mobile application development framework created by Google. It allows developers to create high-performance native apps for iOS, Android, and the web using a single codebase. This means that developers can use Flutter to create apps that run natively on both Android and iOS devices, making it a very powerful tool for mobile app development. Flutter has become increasingly popular in recent years, thanks to its ease of use, flexibility, and ability to create beautiful and highly performant apps. In this book, we will dive into the world of Flutter and learn how to create amazing apps quickly and efficiently.

WHAT IS FLUTTER?

Flutter is a mobile development framework created by Google for building high-performance and visually appealing applications for iOS, Android, and the web. The foundation of Flutter is built on a reactive programming model, enabling fast and easy development of a user interface while allowing developers to focus on creating engaging experiences for their users. Flutter uses Dart programming language, which was also created by Google and is known for its high performance and dynamic features. Dart allows developers to write clean, expressive code that is easy to understand and maintain, making it a popular and efficient language for mobile app development.

WHY CHOOSE FLUTTER FOR APP DEVELOPMENT?

There are many reasons to choose Flutter for app development. Here are just a few: - **Fast Development:** Flutter's hot reload feature allows developers to quickly see changes they make to the app, which makes the development process much faster and efficient. - **Single Codebase:** Flutter allows developers to write a single codebase that runs natively on both Android and iOS devices, meaning that developers can create apps for both platforms in less time. - **High Performance:** Flutter uses Skia graphics library, which means that apps built with Flutter are highly performant. Flutter also uses Dart language, which is known for its speed and connectivity. - **Beautiful UI:** Flutter comes with a wide range of customizable widgets, which makes it easy for developers to create beautiful and polished UI for their apps.

GETTING STARTED WITH FLUTTER DEVELOPMENT ENVIRONMENT

Before we dive deep into the world of Flutter, we need to set up our development environment. To get started with Flutter development, we need the following: - **Flutter SDK:** Flutter SDK is a collection of tools and libraries that we need to develop Flutter apps. You can download the Flutter SDK from the official Flutter website. - **IDE:** For developing Flutter apps, we can use Android Studio, Visual Studio Code, or any other IDE that supports Flutter development. - **Emulator:** We need an emulator to test our apps. We can use the Android Virtual Device (AVD) Manager for Android emulator, and the iOS Simulator for the iOS emulator. Once we have all the tools installed, we can create our first Flutter app and start exploring the world of Flutter!

WHAT IS FLUTTER?

Flutter is an open-source mobile application development framework that allows developers to create high-performance native apps for both iOS and Android platforms with a single codebase. This means that instead of building two separate apps using different programming languages and frameworks, developers can use Flutter to build apps that run natively on both platforms. In essence, Flutter is a complete development kit with pre-built widgets and tools that allows for cross-platform development. One of the most notable features of Flutter is its use of the Dart programming language, which was developed by Google as a modern, easy-to-learn language. This makes it easy for developers to learn and use Flutter, even if they are not familiar with Dart. Flutter is also known for its ″hot reload″ feature, which allows developers to make changes to their app′s code and instantly see those changes reflected in the app without having to recompile the entire codebase. This significantly reduces development time and makes it easier for developers to experiment with different design elements and outcomes. Overall, Flutter is a powerful and innovative platform for mobile app development that offers a wide range of features and benefits to developers. In the next chapter, we will explore the reasons why Flutter is a great choice for app development.

WHY CHOOSE FLUTTER FOR APP DEVELOPMENT?

Flutter is quickly becoming one of the most popular frameworks for developers to use when building mobile applications for iOS and Android. Here are some of the main reasons why Flutter is a great choice for app development:

1. Cross-Platform Compatibility

One of the primary benefits of Flutter is that it allows developers to build apps that will work seamlessly on both iOS and Android platforms. This cross-platform compatibility means that developers can write a single codebase and deploy it to multiple devices, saving both time and money.

2. Native Performance

Flutter apps are built using Google's in-house programming language, Dart, which allows them to run at native speeds on both iOS and Android devices. This means that Flutter apps have the same look and feel as native apps and perform just as well, which is a major selling point for users.

3. Rapid Development

Flutter includes widgets that make it easy for developers to quickly build beautiful and functional user interfaces. It also includes features like hot reload, which allows developers to see changes in real-time, making development faster and more efficient.

4. Open Source Community

As an open-source framework, Flutter has a large community of developers who contribute to its development, making it easy to find support and resources when needed. The community also develops a ton of useful plugins and packages, making it easy for developers to extend the functionality of their apps.

5. Future-Proofed

Flutter is part of Google, which means it's likely to continue to receive heavy investment and development in the future. As a result, developers can be confident that their apps will continue to be supported and upgraded with new features and functionality as the platform evolves.

GETTING STARTED WITH FLUTTER DEVELOPMENT ENVIRONMENT

Before you can start building amazing apps with Flutter, you need to get your development environment set up. Fortunately, setting up Flutter is super easy and can be done in just a few steps. First, you'll need to install the Flutter SDK on your computer. The Flutter team has made this incredibly easy – you can download the SDK bundle from the official Flutter website and extract it to a safe location on your computer. Once you have the SDK installed, you'll need to add Flutter to your system path to be able to use it from the command line. This is a simple one-time setup that will allow you to use the Flutter command-line tools from any directory on your computer. After that, you need to install Android Studio, which is an integrated development environment (IDE) for Android app development. Android

Studio is optional, but recommended, as it provides great tools to make your app development more efficient. Lastly, you'll need to install the Flutter and Dart plugins for Android Studio. These plugins provide support for developing Flutter apps in Android Studio, as well as other useful features like code completion and linting. Congratulations, you're all set up and ready to start developing Flutter apps! In the next chapter, we'll cover the basics of Flutter development and get started building some awesome apps.

Chapter 2: Flutter Basics

Flutter is a cross-platform framework for building high-performance native apps. In this chapter, we will cover the basics of Flutter development, including an overview of Flutter widgets, how to build layouts using Flutter widgets, and how to work with animations and gestures in Flutter.

SUBCHAPTER 2.1 UNDERSTANDING WIDGETS IN FLUTTER

Widgets are the building blocks of a Flutter app. They are used to define the user interface of an app and can range from simple buttons to complex animations. Widgets in Flutter can be classified as either Stateless or Stateful. Stateless Widgets are used to display data that does not change during the course of the application. They are immutable, meaning their properties cannot change once they are built. Stateful Widgets, on the other hand, can change their state during the course of the application. They are mutable and can be updated dynamically with new data or user input.

SUBCHAPTER 2.2 BUILDING LAYOUTS WITH FLUTTER

In Flutter, layout is built using a combination of widgets. The most common layout widget is the Container, which allows you to create a rectangular box that can be styled with different colors, borders, and padding. There are also row and column widgets that allow you to create horizontal and vertical layouts by combining other widgets. Flutter also has a variety of pre-built layout widgets, including GridViews, ListViews, and Stack widgets, which can be used to create more complex layouts.

SUBCHAPTER 2.3 EXPLORING ANIMATION AND GESTURES IN FLUTTER

Flutter provides a powerful set of animation and gesture APIs that allow you to add interactivity to your app. Animations can be used to create smooth transitions between screens or to add visual interest to elements in your app. Gestures, such as tapping, swiping, or pinching, can be used to provide user input and enhance the user experience of your app. In the next chapter, we will explore state management in Flutter and learn how to manage the state of our app using different techniques.

UNDERSTANDING WIDGETS IN FLUTTER

In Flutter, everything is a widget. Widgets are basic building blocks for everything that you see on the screen. So what exactly is a widget? A widget is a part of the user interface that can be drawn onto the screen. This can be anything from a button to a text field. In Flutter, widgets can be stateless or stateful. Stateless widgets are immutable and their state cannot be changed once they are instantiated. On the other hand, stateful widgets have mutable state, which can be modified during the lifetime of the widget. One of the key features of Flutter is that it uses a declarative API. This means that you declare what the UI should look like and Flutter takes care of the rest. You don't have to worry about how the UI is implemented, all you need to do is describe what the UI should look like using widgets. Another important feature of widgets in Flutter is their composability. Widgets can be nested inside each other to create more complex widgets. This allows you to create complex UIs that are easy to manage and maintain. Overall, understanding widgets is crucial to building apps in Flutter. They are the building blocks of the user interface and allow you to create robust and scalable apps.

BUILDING LAYOUTS WITH FLUTTER

One of the most exciting aspects of Flutter is the ease with which complex layouts can be created. Layouts in Flutter are built using widgets, which are the basic building blocks of any Flutter app. In this subchapter, we will explore how to create layouts using Flutter's widget system. Flutter provides a variety of layout widgets, including Column, Row, Flex, GridView, and more. These widgets can be used to create virtually any type of layout. Additionally,

Flutter also provides a handful of predefined widgets for common layout patterns like cards, lists, and tables. One powerful feature of Flutter is the ability to create custom widgets by combining other widgets. This allows you to create complex, reusable UI components that can be used throughout your app. For example, you can create a custom widget for a navigation drawer, which can be easily reused in any screen of the app. To create a layout in Flutter, you simply need to define the hierarchy of widgets that should be displayed on the screen. For example, you might use a Column widget to display a list of items vertically, and then use a ListTile widget for each item in the list. In addition to the built-in layout widgets, Flutter also provides a variety of tools for controlling the positioning and sizing of widgets. For example, you can use the Expanded widget to make a widget take up all available space within a parent widget, or you can use the SizedBox widget to create a fixed-size box. Overall, building layouts with Flutter is a powerful and flexible process that enables developers to create complex, high-quality interfaces with ease. In the next subchapter, we will explore how to add animations and gestures to your layouts.

EXPLORING ANIMATION AND GESTURES IN FLUTTER

Flutter provides a great way to implement animations and gestures in your app. Animations can be used to create a dynamic user interface that reacts to users' actions. Gestures are a way to allow users to interact with the app through touch or mouse events. Flutter provides a built-in animation library that allows the creation of complex animations through simple code. The animation library provides many different types of animations, such as tween animations, physics-based animations, and more. In addition to animations, Flutter also provides support for gestures including tap, double-tap, long-press, drag, and more. With gestures, you can create interactive user interfaces that provide a fluid and natural experience. To implement animations and gestures in Flutter, you can use the AnimationController class to define the duration of the animation and the current value. The Tween class allows you to define the range of values for the animation. You can also use the AnimatedBuilder widget to build animations, and the GestureDetector widget to add gestures to your app. Overall, Flutter provides a powerful toolset for creating animations and gestures that can greatly enhance the user experience of your app. With its easy-to-use animation library and gesture support, Flutter makes it easy to build high-performance native apps for iOS and Android.

Chapter 3: State Management in Flutter

State management is an important concept in Flutter development. It allows your app to keep track of different types of data and update the user interface accordingly. In this chapter, we will explore the different state management techniques used in Flutter.

SUBCHAPTER 3.1: INTRODUCTION TO STATE MANAGEMENT

State management is the process of managing the state of your application in a predictable and maintainable way. In Flutter, state refers to the data that an app uses to determine what to display on the user interface. There are two types of state in Flutter: widget state and application state. Widget state refers to the state that belongs to a specific widget. This state is ephemeral, meaning it only exists as long as the widget is alive. Any changes to the widget state will trigger a rebuild of the widget. Application state, on the other hand, is the state of the entire application. This state can persist even if the widget that created it no longer exists. Application state can be used to manage data such as user settings, user preferences, and other data that needs to be persisted across multiple screens or sessions.

SUBCHAPTER 3.2: USING SETSTATE AND INHERITED WIDGETS

One way to manage widget state in Flutter is by using the `setState` method. This method is used to modify the state of a widget and trigger a rebuild. Whenever you call `setState`, Flutter will rebuild the widget and its children, updating the user interface to reflect the new state. Another way to manage widget state in Flutter is by using inherited widgets. An inherited widget is a widget that provides data to its children. This data can be accessed by any widget that is a descendant of the inherited widget. Inherited widgets are commonly used for managing data that needs to be shared between multiple widgets, such as theme data or localization data.

SUBCHAPTER 3.3:
IMPLEMENTING REDUX IN FLUTTER

Redux is a popular state management library that originated in the React community. It is based on the principles of functional programming and provides a predictable way to manage application state. Redux can be used in Flutter using the `flutter_redux` package. The basic principle of Redux is that the application state is represented by a single store. The store is a data structure that contains all the application data. Changes to the state are made by dispatching actions, which are plain JavaScript objects that describe the state mutation. Reducers are functions that take the current state and an action, and return a new state. In Flutter, the equivalent of a reducer is a function that takes the current state and an action, and returns a new state. The state is then passed to the widget tree using an inherited widget.

Overall, Redux provides a powerful and maintainable way to manage application state in Flutter.

INTRODUCTION TO STATE MANAGEMENT

State management is a fundamental concept in Flutter application development that involves managing the current state of the user interface. In simple terms, state is information that can be used to describe a Flutter app's user interface at any given moment in time. In Flutter, state management refers to the process of updating the state of the user interface when events occur in the app. This can include user interactions, changes in data, or other actions that require the user interface to be updated. There are many different approaches to state management in Flutter, and the best approach will often depend on the specific needs of your app. Some common approaches to state management include using StatefulWidget,

InheritedWidget, and Providers. Understanding state management is critical to building high-performance, scalable Flutter applications. In the next few subchapters, we will explore different state management techniques and help you decide which approach is right for your app.

USING SETSTATE AND INHERITED WIDGETS

State management is an essential part of modern app development, and Flutter provides two primary ways of managing state within an app: the setState method and the Inherited Widget. The setState method is a straightforward way to modify state within a widget. It is called whenever a user action triggers a state transition, and it should only be used within small widgets that are directly related to the state change. The reason for this is that it rebuilds the widget tree each time it is called, which can be computationally expensive if there are many widgets. On the other hand, Inherited

Widgets provide a way to manage state across the entire app and share state between widgets that are not necessarily related in the widget tree. This makes it much easier to manage complex state, such as user authentication or application settings. One significant advantage of using the Inherited Widget approach is that it reduces the amount of boilerplate code that is required to manage state within an app. Instead of passing state down the widget tree manually, the Inherited Widget does this automatically. In addition to managing application state, the Inherited Widget also provides a mechanism for rebuilding the UI when the state changes. This ensures that the user interface is always synchronized with the underlying state of the application. Understanding how to use both setState and Inherited Widgets is essential for any Flutter developer who wants to build robust, high-performance apps that can scale to meet the needs of a large user base. With these tools in your arsenal, you can build apps that are easy to maintain, provide a great user experience, and grow with the needs of your users. In the next chapter, we will explore implementing Redux in Flutter to further enhance your state management options.

IMPLEMENTING REDUX IN FLUTTER

State management plays a crucial role in building scalable and maintainable applications, and using Redux can make it much easier. Redux is a state management library that helps to manage the state of an application efficiently. It is widely used in web development and has gained popularity in mobile app development, particularly in Flutter. In Redux, the state of an application is stored in a single source of truth called a store. When an event or an action occurs, a reducer function is called to update the store, and the UI is updated accordingly. This approach makes the data flow easier to track and debug, especially in large applications. To use Redux in Flutter, you need to install the flutter_redux package first. It provides the necessary components to integrate Flutter with Redux. Once installed, you can create a Store object to hold the state of your application. The Store is the central hub of your application's state. Next, you need to create reducers. A reducer is a pure function that defines how the state of the application should change when an action is dispatched. Reducers take the current state and action as input parameters and return the updated state. You can combine multiple reducers into a single reducer using combineReducers function provided by the flutter_redux package. After creating reducers, you can create actions to dispatch events. An action is a plain Dart object that contains the minimum amount of information to describe what happened in the application. Actions are dispatched by calling the dispatch() function on the Store object. When an action is dispatched, it is sent to all reducers, which update the state of the application as necessary. Finally, you can access the store in your widgets using the StoreProvider widget provided by flutter_redux. This widget automatically updates your UI based on the state changes in the Store. You can also use the Connect widget to map specific parts of your Store to your widgets. In summary, using Redux in Flutter can make state management more organized and easier to maintain. It provides a clear and efficient data flow between your application's components, especially in large applications. With the flutter_redux package, integrating Redux into your Flutter app is easy and straightforward.

Chapter 4: APIs and Networking in Flutter

Communicating with external APIs is an essential part of app development, and Flutter has built-in support for making HTTP requests and handling responses. In this chapter, we will explore how to retrieve data from various APIs and parse the responses in Flutter.

SUBCHAPTER 4.1 MAKING API CALLS IN FLUTTER

Making API calls involves sending HTTP requests to a server. In Flutter, this can be achieved using the `http` package, which provides functions for making various types of HTTP requests. To make a GET request, for example, you can use the `get` method of the `http` package: ``` import 'package: http/http.dart' as http; Future fetchData() async { final response = await http.get(Uri.parse('https://jsonplaceholder.t ypicode.com/posts')); print(response.body); } ``` In this example, we are using the `http.get` function to retrieve data from an external API. The argument to the `http.get` function is a `Uri` that specifies the URL of the API endpoint we want to call.

SUBCHAPTER 4.2 HANDLING API RESPONSES IN FLUTTER

After making an API call, we need to handle the response data. API responses are often encoded in JSON format, and we can use the `dart:convert` library to decode the JSON response into a Dart object. ``` import 'dart:convert'; import 'package:http/http.dart' as http; Future fetchData() async { final response = await http.get(Uri.parse('https://jsonplaceholder.typicode.com/posts')); final List data = jsonDecode(response.body); for (final item in data) { print(item['title']); } } ``` In this example, we are using the `jsonDecode` function from the `dart:convert` library to convert the response body into a list of dynamic objects. We can then iterate over the list and access the properties of each object.

SUBCHAPTER 4.3
IMPLEMENTING
AUTHENTICATION WITH
FIREBASE IN FLUTTER

Firebase is a popular backend platform that provides various services for app development, including authentication, database, and cloud functions. Flutter provides a plugin for integrating with Firebase, making it easy to use Firebase services in your app. To use Firebase Authentication in your app, you need to first add Firebase to your project and configure the necessary settings. You can then use the `firebase_auth` package to interact with Firebase Authentication. ``` import 'package: firebase_auth/firebase_auth.dart'; final FirebaseAuth _auth = FirebaseAuth.instance; Future loginUser(String email, String password) async { try { final UserCredential userCredential = await _auth.signInWithEmailAndPassword(

email: email, password: password,); final User user = userCredential.user; print('User with email ${user.email} has signed in'); } on FirebaseAuthException catch (e) { print('Error: $e'); } } ``` In this example, we are using the `signInWithEmailAndPassword` method to authenticate a user with an email and password. The method returns a `UserCredential` object, which contains information about the authenticated user. We can then access the `user` property of the `UserCredential` object to get the user's email address. Overall, API and networking integration is a crucial aspect of app development, and Flutter provides solid support for accessing external APIs and handling responses. With the right tools and techniques, you can easily fetch data from various APIs and use it to create engaging apps.

MAKING API CALLS IN FLUTTER

In today's connected world, almost all mobile apps need to interact with server-side data. To achieve this in Flutter, we use API calls to fetch data from the server and render it in the app. In this chapter, we will explore how to make API calls in Flutter using different libraries and methods available. We will start with the basics of fetching data from a REST API endpoint, and then dive deeper into more advanced features like authentication and error handling. With Flutter's reactive programming model, we can easily render server data in our views by just updating the state of our widgets. By the end of this chapter, you will have a good understanding of how to fetch data from an API endpoint and render it in a Flutter app.

HANDLING API RESPONSES IN FLUTTER

In the world of app development, APIs have become an integral part of any product that relies on external data sources. In Flutter, making API calls is a straightforward process, but it's equally important to handle the responses that come back from the server gracefully and efficiently. When making an API request in Flutter, the server will respond with a set of data that needs to be processed. The response can contain a variety of data types such as JSON, XML, or plain text. To handle the response, you can use the `http` package that Flutter provides. The package has a built-in support for making HTTP requests and handling responses. After sending a request, the package provides a `Response` object that contains the server's response including the data and the status code. One common method to handle the response is to parse the data into a Dart object using JSON serialization or deserialization. You can use the `dart:convert` package that comes built-in with Flutter to convert the JSON data into a Dart object. On the other hand, if the response contains an error status code, the server has encountered an issue while processing the request. For instance, if the server is down, the HTTP status code would be 503. In this scenario, you should display an error message to the user or retry the operation at a later time. In summary, understanding how to handle API responses in Flutter is critical to building high-performing apps. By using the `http` package and processing response data efficiently, you can create apps that deliver high-quality user experiences.

IMPLEMENTING AUTHENTICATION WITH FIREBASE IN FLUTTER

Firebase is a mobile and web application development platform that provides developers the tools to build high-quality applications. With Firebase, developers can focus on building the core features of their application by leveraging pre-built services like analytics, database, cloud storage, and authentication. In this subchapter, we will be focusing on how to implement user authentication using Firebase in your Flutter app. User authentication is a crucial part of any app that requires user data to be stored and accessed securely. Firebase provides an easy and secure way to handle user authentication in Flutter with just a few lines of code. To get started, you need to create a Firebase project and configure the Firebase SDK in your Flutter app. The configuration process includes adding the Firebase SDK to your project and connecting your app to Firebase. Once that's done, you can start implementing user authentication with Firebase in your Flutter app. Firebase provides several authentication methods like email and password authentication, Google authentication, Facebook authentication, Twitter authentication, and more. For example, to implement email and password authentication, you need to create a form with two input fields for email and password. Then, you can use the `signInWithEmailAndPassword` method provided by the Firebase authentication API to sign in the user. ```dart final FirebaseAuth _auth = FirebaseAuth.instance; Future signInWithEmail(String email, String password) async { try { UserCredential userCredential = await _auth.signInWithEmailAndPassword(email : email, password: password); User user = userCredential.user; return user.uid; } on FirebaseAuthException catch (e) { if (e.code == 'user-not-found') { return 'No user found for that email.'; } else if (e.code == 'wrong-password') { return 'Wrong password provided for that user.'; } } } ``` Similarly, you can use the `createUserWithEmailAndPassword` method to create a new user account. ```dart Future registerWithEmail(String email, String password) async { try {

```
UserCredential userCredential = await
_auth.createUserWithEmailAndPassword(
email: email, password: password); User
user = userCredential.user; return user.uid;
} on FirebaseAuthException catch (e) { if
(e.code == 'weak-password') { return 'The
password provided is too weak.'; } else if
(e.code == 'email-already-in-use') { return
'The account already exists for that email.';
} } catch (e) { return 'Error: $e'; } } ```
```

Firebase also allows you to implement custom authentication with the Firebase Authentication API. Custom authentication enables your app to integrate with your own authentication system or a third-party system. In conclusion, implementing user authentication with Firebase in your Flutter app is an important aspect of building a secure and reliable app. Firebase provides an easy and seamless way to handle user authentication without worrying about the backend infrastructure.

Chapter 5: Flutter Packages and Plugins

When developing an application, it's crucial to have access to the best tools and features that can streamline the process for you. That's where Flutter Packages and Plugins come in. They provide a vast range of functionalities, making it easier to build complex applications with less code.

INTRODUCTION TO PACKAGES AND PLUGINS

Flutter Packages are reusable sets of codes that offer a wide variety of functions. It's a collection of classes, files, configurations, and assets that you can easily integrate into your project. These packages are like libraries with predefined functionality. You can search for them in the Pub.dev repository using the command line or in your project's pubspec.yaml file. Plugins, on the other hand, are native features that allow applications to access the device's hardware or platform-specific components. Flutter Plugins are built on top of these native features and allow for integration with the Dart programming language. For instance, plugins can help you access the device's camera, storage, location services, and many other native functionalities.

USING EXTERNAL PACKAGES IN FLUTTER

Using external packages in Flutter is a straightforward process. You need to add the package to your project's pubspec.yaml file that specifies all dependencies that you want to use. When you add the package, the Flutter tool will automatically download and manage the package's version compatibility and dependencies. Once you've added the package, you can import it into your code and start using the functionality provided by the package. For instance, if you're using a package like `flutter_launcher_icons`, you can easily add the package to your project, configure your icons, and generate them using the command-line interface.

DEVELOPING CUSTOM PACKAGES FOR FLUTTER

If you can't find a package that provides the functionality you need, you can develop your own Flutter package. Creating your package is an excellent way to reuse code between multiple projects, share code with other developers or the open-source community. Developing a package involves creating a new Dart package in a separate directory and then adding your Dart files and assets. You can also define configurations and provide examples in the package to help other developers understand how to use it.

Conclusion

Flutter Packages and Plugins provide developers with massive resources to make the development process more accessible and efficient. Whether you're building simple or complex applications, there is always a package or plugin that will help you add the required functionality to your project. You can use popular packages developed by Google and other developers or create your packages if you can't find a suitable package.

INTRODUCTION TO PACKAGES AND PLUGINS

Flutter is highly customizable and extensible, thanks to its packages and plugins system. In this chapter, we will dive into what packages and plugins are and how they can be leveraged to help you build your Flutter app better and faster than ever before. In simple terms, packages are collections of code that other developers have made available to the public for use in their own apps. A package might contain highly specialized code for specific tasks, such as date formatting or image

45

manipulation. Plugins, on the other hand, provide access to platform-specific functionality that isn't readily available in the Flutter SDK. For example, plugins can provide access to a device's camera or allow your app to integrate with a specific social media platform. Flutter has a vast collection of packages and plugins that can be easily added to your project via the pubspec.yaml file. The pubspec.yaml file is where you declare the dependencies for your project, including any packages or plugins that your project needs to run. In the next subchapter, we will discuss how to use external packages in your project to add functionality that would otherwise need to be implemented from scratch.

USING EXTERNAL PACKAGES IN FLUTTER

Flutter has a vast range of external packages and plugins that can help you add advanced features and capabilities to your apps. These packages contain pre-written code that you can use to save time and reduce the amount of code you have to write from scratch. To use an external package in your Flutter project, you need to add it to your project's *pubspec.yaml* file. The pubspec file is a configuration file that lists all the dependencies for your project. Here are the steps to add an external package to your project:

Step 1: Find the package

You can search for packages on the official Flutter package website (pub.dev). On this site, you can find packages that have been developed and maintained by the Flutter community.

Step 2: Add the package to the pubspec file

After finding the package you want to use, you can add it to your project's *pubspec.yaml* file. Here's an example: dependencies:

my_package: ^1.0.0 The *my_package* is

the name of the package and the ^1.0.0 specifies the package version. The ^ symbol in front of the version number tells Flutter to fetch the latest version of the package within the 1.x.x range.

Step 3: Run pub get

After adding the package to your pubspec file, you need to run the *pub get* command in your terminal. This command downloads and installs the package and all its dependencies. Once you've completed these steps, you can start using the package in your code by importing it like this: import 'package: my_package/my_package.dart';

You can now use the classes and methods provided by the package in your code. Using external packages can boost your productivity and help you create more complex and advanced apps in less time. However, it's essential to choose reliable packages with good documentation and active development. Additionally, you should be aware of the dependencies that the package brings and avoid adding too many packages as it can slow down your app's performance.

DEVELOPING CUSTOM PACKAGES FOR FLUTTER

Flutter packages are a great way to easily add additional functionality to your app. However, what if you need a specific functionality that is not available in any of the existing packages? That's where developing custom packages for Flutter comes in. Developing your own Flutter package can seem daunting at first, but it's actually quite simple once you get the hang of it. Here are the basic steps to get started:

Step 1: Create a new Flutter package project

To start creating your own Flutter package, first create a new Flutter package project by running the following command in your terminal: ``` flutter create --template=package my_package_name ```

This will create a new directory for your package and add the necessary files and folders.

Step 2: Add your code to the package

Next, add your code to the `lib` folder in your package. This can include any combination of Dart code, assets, and resources. Make sure to properly structure your code to make it easy to use for other developers.

Step 3: Add a `pubspec.yaml` file

The `pubspec.yaml` file is the configuration file for your package. Here, you can add dependencies, specify the package name, version, and other metadata such as author and description.

Step 4: Publish your package to pub.dev

Once you have created your package, you can publish it to pub.dev, which is the official package repository for Flutter. Others can then easily use your package in their own projects. To publish to pub.dev, first sign up for an account on the website. Then, run the following command in your terminal: ``` flutter packages pub publish ``` This will publish your package to pub.dev.

Step 5: Keep your package up-to-date

Once you have published your package, it's important to keep it up-to-date with any changes or new features. Continuously updating your package will ensure that it remains relevant and useful for others to use in their own projects. In conclusion, developing custom packages for Flutter is a great way to share your code with others and add valuable functionality to the Flutter ecosystem. Don't be afraid to dive in and start creating your own packages!

Chapter 6: Advanced Flutter Concepts

SUBCHAPTER 6.1 BUILDING CUSTOM WIDGETS AND ANIMATIONS IN FLUTTER

As you become more experienced with Flutter, you'll likely want to create your own custom widgets and animations to give your apps a unique look and feel. Luckily, Flutter provides a powerful set of tools that make it easy to create custom widgets and animations. At the heart of creating custom widgets in Flutter are two classes: the `StatelessWidget` and the `StatefulWidget`. The `StatelessWidget` is a simple widget that does not change over time. It returns the same UI every time it is called. In contrast, the `StatefulWidget` is used for widgets that can change over time. It has two classes, the

`State` and the `StatefulWidget`. The `StatefulWidget` defines the widget itself, while the `State` class maintains the state of the widget between builds. When building custom animations, you can use Flutter's built-in animation controller to control the animation playback. The animation controller provides a simple way to update animation values at a set interval and interpolate those values over the course of the animation. You can then use the interpolated values to update your widget's user interface.

SUBCHAPTER 6.2
IMPLEMENTING PUSH NOTIFICATIONS IN FLUTTER

Push notifications are a crucial aspect of modern mobile app development, as they allow users to stay informed even when they're not using your app. In Flutter, you can implement push notifications using Firebase Cloud Messaging (FCM), which allows you to send notifications to users even when your app is not open. To implement push notifications in your Flutter app, you first need to create a Firebase project and enable FCM. Once you have done that, you can use the `firebase_messaging` Flutter plugin to receive and handle push notifications. The plugin provides callbacks that are triggered when the app receives a notification, allowing you to display a notification in your app's user interface or perform some other action.

SUBCHAPTER 6.3 DEPLOYING FLUTTER APPS TO THE APP STORE AND GOOGLE PLAY STORE

Once you have built your Flutter app, you'll need to deploy it to the app stores. Deploying to the app stores can be a complex process, but Flutter provides tools to simplify it. To deploy your app to the App Store or Google Play Store, you first need to create an app manifest and bundle your app's binary file. You also need to sign your app with a valid certificate. Flutter provides a tool called `flutter build` that can automate much of this process for you. After you have bundled and signed your app, you can then submit it to the app stores for review. The review process can take several days to a few weeks, so be sure to plan accordingly when scheduling your app release. Once your app is approved, it will be available for download on the app store.# Building Custom Widgets and Animations in Flutter Flutter makes it easy to build custom widgets and animations that give your app a unique look and feel. Custom widgets are a great way to create reusable and self-contained UI components that can be used throughout your app. Animations, on the other hand, can add interactivity and delight to your app. ## Creating Custom Widgets Creating a custom widget in Flutter is simple. All you need to do is extend the `StatelessWidget` or `StatefulWidget` class and implement the `build` method. The `build` method is where you define the widget's layout and behavior. For example, let's say you want to create a custom button widget that has a different background color and text color than the default `RaisedButton`. Here's how you would do it: ```dart class CustomButton extends StatelessWidget { final String label; final VoidCallback onPressed; final Color backgroundColor; final Color textColor; const CustomButton({ Key key, @required this.label, @required this.onPressed, this.backgroundColor, this.textColor, }) : super(key: key); @override Widget build(BuildContext context) { return RaisedButton(onPressed: onPressed, child: Text(label), color: backgroundColor ?? Theme.of(context).primaryColor, textColor: textColor ?? Colors.white,); } } ``` In the example above, we've created a `CustomButton` widget with four parameters: `label`, `onPressed`, `backgroundColor`, and `textColor`. We've also set default values for `backgroundColor` and `textColor` in case they're not provided. In the `build` method, we're returning a `RaisedButton` widget with the provided `onPressed` callback and `label` text. We're also using the provided `backgroundColor` and `textColor` values if they exist, or falling back to the default primary color and white, respectively. ## Creating Animations Animations can add life to your app and make it more engaging for users. Flutter makes it easy to create animations with its built-in animation classes and widgets. For example, let's say you want to create a custom animation that rotates an icon when the user taps on it. Here's how you would do it: ```dart class RotateIcon extends StatefulWidget { final IconData icon; const RotateIcon({Key key, @required this.icon}) : super(key: key); @override _RotateIconState createState() => _RotateIconState(); } class _RotateIconState extends State with SingleTickerProviderStateMixin { AnimationController _controller; Animation _animation; @override void initState() { super.initState(); _controller =

```
AnimationController( vsync: this, duration:
const   Duration(milliseconds:   500),   );
_animation = Tween( begin: 0, end: 1,
).animate(_controller);   }  @override  void
dispose()         {         _controller.dispose();
super.dispose();    }    @override   Widget
build(BuildContext   context)   {    return
GestureDetector(    onTap:    ()    {    if
(_controller.status                        ==
AnimationStatus.completed)               {
_controller.reverse();      }     else    {
_controller.forward();      }     },     child:
AnimatedBuilder(  animation:  _animation,
builder:   (context,   child)   {    return
Transform.rotate( angle: _animation.value *
2 * pi, child: Icon(widget.icon), ); }, ), ); } }
```
``` In the example above, we've created a
custom `RotateIcon` widget that takes an
`icon` parameter. In the `initState` method,
we've created an `AnimationController` and
set up a basic animation with a duration of
500 milliseconds. We've also set up a
`GestureDetector` that triggers the
animation when the user taps on the widget.
In the `build` method, we're returning an
```

`AnimatedBuilder` widget that rebuilds whenever the `_animation` value changes. We're using the `_animation` value to calculate the rotation angle for the `Transform.rotate` widget, which is rotating the provided `Icon` widget. ## Conclusion Custom widgets and animations are just a few examples of the powerful features that Flutter offers. By understanding how to create custom widgets and animations, you can create unique and delightful experiences for your users. In the next subchapter, we'll explore how to implement push notifications in Flutter.

IMPLEMENTING PUSH NOTIFICATIONS IN FLUTTER

Push notifications are a crucial feature in any modern mobile application. They allow developers to keep users engaged by providing timely updates and reminders. Flutter makes it easy to implement push notifications in your app. In this subchapter, we will cover the basics of push notifications and show you how to implement them in Flutter. The first step in implementing push notifications is to set up a push notification provider. In Flutter, we have the option to use Firebase Cloud Messaging (FCM) as our provider. To get started, you will need to create an FCM project in the Firebase console. Once you have done that, you can add the necessary dependencies to your Flutter app. Next, you will need to configure your app to receive push notifications. This involves registering your app with FCM and obtaining a registration token. You can then use this token to send push notifications to the specific device. In Flutter, we can use the firebase_messaging package to handle push notifications. This package provides a FirebaseMessaging object that we can use to set up our push notifications. We can use the getToken() method of this object to retrieve the registration token for the device. To handle incoming notifications, we can implement a FirebaseMessaging.onMessage() listener.

This listener will be called whenever a new message is received while the app is running. We can also implement a FirebaseMessaging.onBackgroundMessage( ) listener to handle notifications when the app is in the background. Overall, implementing push notifications in Flutter is a straightforward process. By leveraging Firebase Cloud Messaging and the firebase_messaging package, we can provide a seamless push notification experience for our users.Subchapter 6.3: Deploying Flutter Apps to the App Store and Google Play Store Congratulations, you've built an awesome Flutter app! Now, it's time to share it with the world. In this subchapter, you'll learn how to deploy your app to the App Store and Google Play Store. Deploying to the App Store To deploy your app to the App Store, you'll need to have an Apple Developer account. Once you have that, you'll need to navigate to the App Store Connect dashboard and create a new app. From there, you can upload your app and submit it for review. Before you submit your app, make sure to test it thoroughly and ensure it meets all of Apple's guidelines. This includes adhering to their design guidelines, handling in-app purchases properly, and ensuring your app is stable and doesn't crash. Once your app is approved by Apple, it will be available for download on the App Store. Congratulations, you've officially launched your app! Deploying to Google Play Store To deploy your app to the Google Play Store, you'll need to have a Google Play Developer account. Once you have that, you can create a new app and upload your APK file. Like with the App Store, it's important to test your app thoroughly before submitting it. Make sure it meets Google's guidelines, has proper privacy policies, and doesn't contain any malicious code. Once you submit your app, it will go through a review process. If it's approved, it will be available for download on the Google Play Store. Conclusion Deploying your Flutter app to the App Store and Google Play Store is an exciting moment in the app development process. Make sure you follow all of Apple and Google's guidelines and thoroughly test your app before submitting it. Once it's live, you can sit back and watch your app reach a global audience!

Chapter 7: Best Practices for Flutter Development

Flutter is an amazing framework that can help you build high-performance native apps for both iOS and Android. But to make the most of Flutter, it's important to follow best practices.

SUBCHAPTER 7.1: WRITING CLEAN CODE IN FLUTTER

One of the most important best practices in Flutter development is to write clean and maintainable code. Clean code is easy to read, easy to understand, and easy to modify, which makes it much easier to maintain your codebase over time. To write clean code in Flutter, you should follow some guidelines:

1. Use Descriptive Variable and Function Names

Use meaningful names for your variables and functions. This makes it easier for other developers to understand your code. Avoid single-letter variable names or generic names like 'data' or 'temp'. Instead, use descriptive names like 'userProfile', 'listOfContacts', or 'fetchUserDataFromServer'.

2. Follow the DRY (Don't Repeat Yourself) Principle

Avoid duplicating code. If you find yourself writing similar code in multiple places, extract that code into a separate function or class and reuse it. This not only saves time but also makes it easier to maintain your codebase.

3. Use Comments Sparingly and Effectively

Comments can be helpful in understanding code, but they should be used sparingly and only when necessary. Avoid cluttering your code with comments, and focus on writing self-documenting code instead. When you do use comments, they should be clear, concise, and explain why something is written that way, not what it does.

SUBCHAPTER 7.2: OPTIMIZING PERFORMANCE IN FLUTTER

Flutter apps can be incredibly fast and performant, but to achieve this, you need to optimize your code for performance. Here are some tips for optimizing your Flutter app's performance:

1. Use Stateless Widgets Whenever Possible

Stateless widgets are faster and more performant than stateful ones. If a widget doesn't need to change over time, use a stateless widget instead of a stateful one.

2. Minimize the use of the setState function

The setState function comes with a performance cost, especially when called multiple times in a short period. It's essential to use it only when required, instead, you can use provider, or ChangeNotifier if you need to update the state of your widget.

3. Avoid Making Unnecessary API Calls

API calls can be slow, especially if your app is making lots of them. Try to minimize the number of API calls your app makes, combine them into fewer calls whenever possible, and use caching to avoid making the same call multiple times.

SUBCHAPTER 7.3: DEBUGGING AND TESTING FLUTTER APPS

Debugging and testing are crucial parts of app development, and Flutter provides fantastic tools to make this easier. Here are some tips for debugging and testing your Flutter app:

1. Use DevTools to Debug Your App

DevTools is a powerful debugging tool that you can use to analyze and debug your Flutter app. You can use it to profile your app's performance, identify rendering issues, and inspect the widget tree.

2. Write Unit Tests for Your Codebase

Unit tests are automated tests that verify that individual parts of your app work as expected. You can use the built-in testing framework in Flutter, and regularly write these tests to ensure your codebase is stable and reliable.

3. Use Flutter Driver for End-to-End Testing

End-to-end testing involves testing your app as a whole, including user interactions and screen navigations. Flutter Driver is a tool that can help you automate end-to-end testing in Flutter. By simulating user interactions, you can identify bugs and issues that would be difficult to find through other testing methods.

CONCLUSION

Following best practices can help you build better-quality Flutter apps faster and more efficiently. Writing clean and maintainable code, optimizing performance, and debugging and testing your app are essential parts of building a successful Flutter app.

WRITING CLEAN CODE IN FLUTTER

Writing clean code is crucial to producing high-quality and maintainable Flutter applications. Clean code is code that is easy to read, understand, and modify. In Flutter, clean code can greatly simplify the development process by reducing the likelihood of errors and improving the overall quality of your codebase. Here are some tips for writing clean code in Flutter:

Properly Indent Your Code

Properly indenting your code makes it easier to read and follow. Use the standard indentation conventions for your language. In Flutter, the standard is four spaces.

Use Descriptive Naming Conventions

Use meaningful and descriptive names for your variables, functions, and classes. This will make it easier to understand your code, and will make it easier to maintain in the future.

Keep Functions Short and Focused

Functions should do one thing and do it well. Keep functions short and focused. This makes them easier to understand and modify. If a function becomes too long, consider breaking it up into smaller, more focused functions.

Comment Your Code

Comment your code to explain complex logic and algorithms. Comments can make it easier to understand code, especially for other developers who may be working on the same codebase.

Use Error Handling

Always include error handling in your code. Error handling helps ensure that your application can recover gracefully from errors and faults, and can prevent problems from getting worse. Following these tips will help you produce clean and maintainable code in Flutter. Incorporating these practices into your development workflow can greatly improve the quality of your codebase, and make it easier to work with in the long run.

SUBCHAPTER 7.2 OPTIMIZING PERFORMANCE IN FLUTTER

When it comes to building mobile apps, performance is a crucial factor that can make or break the success of your product. With Flutter, you can build beautiful, high-quality apps that can run smoothly on both iOS and Android devices. However, there are some tips and tricks that you can implement to optimize your app's performance and provide a seamless user experience. Here are some best practices for optimizing the performance of your Flutter app:

1. Reduce the Size of Images

Images can significantly impact your app's performance, especially when they are large. To avoid this issue, make sure to reduce the size of your images before including them in your app. You can use tools like Adobe Photoshop or Gimp to compress the images and reduce their file size without compromising their quality.

2. Use the ListView.builder Widget

If your app requires displaying a large list of items, it's recommended to use the ListView.builder widget. This widget efficiently creates and recycles list items as needed. This can help reduce memory usage and improve app performance.

3. Implement lazy loading

Lazy loading is a technique that loads data and resources on demand rather than all at once. This can be especially useful for data-intensive apps with large amounts of data. By implementing lazy loading, you can improve your app's startup time and overall performance.

4. Minimize the use of Animations

While animations can provide a great user experience, they can also negatively impact your app's performance. It's important to minimize the use of animations, especially complex ones. If possible, use simple, lightweight animations that don't put too much load on the device's CPU.

5. Profile your App

Profiling is the process of analyzing your app's performance to identify potential bottlenecks and areas for improvement. This can help you identify areas where you can optimize your app's performance. Flutter provides tools like the Observatory and the Flutter Performance Toolkit, which can help you profile your app and identify performance issues. By following these best practices, you can optimize the performance of your Flutter app and provide a seamless user experience. Remember, the key to building a successful app is not only its functionality but also its performance and usability.Debugging and testing are critical steps in app development that cannot be ignored. It is essential to ensure that all bugs are identified and resolved before an app is launched to the public. In this subchapter, we will discuss various debugging and testing techniques you can use to build high-quality Flutter apps. ## Debugging Flutter Apps Debugging is the process of identifying and locating errors or bugs in a program. Flutter offers various debugging tools to help you identify and resolve bugs in your app quickly. The most common debugging method used in Flutter is print statements. You can use print statements to output information about variables or code that you suspect might be causing a problem. Another useful debugging tool is the Flutter Inspector. This tool provides a visual representation of your app and allows you to inspect each widget's properties at runtime. You can use it to identify issues in real-time, such as layout issues or incorrect widget properties. You can use the Flutter

Inspector by selecting the "Open DevTools" button in the Flutter toolbar or by pressing "Alt + Shift + X" in the Flutter IDE. The Dart Observatory is another powerful debugging tool that allows you to observe and monitor the memory usage and CPU performance of your app. You can also use it to execute Dart code during runtime, which can help you identify and fix issues with your app. You can access the Dart Observatory by selecting the "Open Observatory" button in the Flutter toolbar or by pressing "Alt + Shift + O" in the Flutter IDE. ## Testing Flutter Apps Testing is the validation of an app to ensure that it meets the specified requirements and functions correctly. Flutter provides developers with several testing options, including unit testing, widget testing, and integration testing. Unit testing involves testing individual functions or modules of your app in isolation. This process ensures that each function is working correctly and efficiently without interacting with other parts of the app. Widget testing is the process of testing individual widgets of an app to ensure that they work correctly. Integration testing, on the other hand, involves testing all parts of an app together to ensure they interact seamlessly. Flutter offers integrated support for testing using the Flutter test framework. This framework provides a set of test widgets that can help you create and run tests. You can also use third-party testing libraries such as Mockito, which allows you to create mock objects for testing. In conclusion, debugging and testing are crucial in app development. They ensure that your app is working correctly and efficiently without any issues. Flutter provides various debugging and testing tools to help you identify and resolve bugs in your app, ensuring a smooth user experience.

Conclusion and Next Steps

Congratulations on making it this far in the book! By now, you should have a solid understanding of Flutter and how to use it to build high-performance native apps for iOS and Android. But the journey doesn't have to end here. In this final chapter, we'll review some key concepts and provide some next steps for further learning and development.

REVIEW OF KEY CONCEPTS

Throughout this book, we covered a lot of ground. We started with an introduction to Flutter, discussing what it is and why it's a great choice for mobile app development. We then moved on to the basics, learning about widgets, layouts, animations, and gestures. We explored state management and how to make API calls and handle responses in Flutter. We also talked about packages and plugins and how to build custom widgets and animations. Finally, we reviewed best practices for development and testing. One of the most important concepts to remember is the importance of writing clean code. This will not only make your app more maintainable in the long run, but it will also help improve performance.

Another key concept is the use of state management to manage user interactions and keep the app responsive.

NEXT STEPS

Now that you have a good understanding of Flutter, there are several next steps you can take to continue your learning and development. Here are some ideas: 1. Build more apps: The best way to improve your skills is to keep building more apps. Try building different types of apps with varying complexity. 2. Join the Flutter community: There are numerous online communities and forums where Flutter developers share their knowledge and learn from each other. Join these communities, ask questions, and collaborate with other developers. 3. Attend meetups and conferences: Attend local meetups or national conferences to learn more about new features and best practices. You may even find opportunities to network and form collaborations. 4. Read up on advanced concepts: There are many advanced concepts in Flutter, such as custom painting, platform channels, and integrating machine learning. Read up on some of these topics to expand your knowledge.

FINAL THOUGHTS

Flutter is an exciting technology that's transforming the world of mobile app development. With its ease of use, fast development time, and excellent performance, Flutter is quickly becoming the go-to framework for building high-performance native apps for both iOS and Android. We hope that this book has provided you with the knowledge and skills needed to become a Flutter Pro. So go forth, build great apps, and have fun!

SUBCHAPTER 8.1: REVIEW OF KEY CONCEPTS

Congratulations, you have reached the final chapter of this book! We have covered a lot of ground, so let's take a moment to review some of the key concepts we have learned about Flutter. Firstly, we started with an introduction to Flutter, discussing what it is and why it has become popular in recent years. We then went on to learn about the Flutter development environment and how to set it up. Next, we explored widgets in Flutter and how they are used to build UI layouts. We saw how animation and gestures can be added to widgets, making the UI more interactive and engaging. We then moved on to state management in Flutter, discussing the different options available and how to use them effectively. We also looked at APIs and networking in Flutter and how to handle responses from them. In the fifth chapter, we learned about packages and plugins and saw how they can be used to add additional functionality to our Flutter apps. We also looked at some advanced concepts, such as building custom widgets and animations and implementing push notifications. Finally, we discussed best practices for Flutter development, such as writing clean code, optimizing performance, and debugging and testing our apps. Overall, this book has covered a lot of ground and provided you with the knowledge and skills necessary to build high-performance native apps for iOS and Android using Flutter. We hope that you have found this book informative and useful, and we wish you all the best in your Flutter development journey. Thank you for reading "Become a Flutter Pro: Build High-Performance Native Apps for iOS and Android".